Basketball

GETTING THE EDGE: CONDITIONING, INJURIES, AND LEGAL & ILLICIT DRUGS

Baseball and Softball

Basketball

Cheerleading

Extreme Sports

Football

Gymnastics

Hockey

Lacrosse

Martial Arts

Soccer

Track & Field

Volleyball

Weightlifting

Wrestling

SLAM DUNK
BASKETBALL

Basketball

by Gabrielle Vanderhoof

Mason Crest Publishers

MASON CREST PUBLISHERS INC.
370 Reed Road
Broomall, Pennsylvania 19008
(866)MCP-BOOK (toll free)
www.masoncrest.com

First Printing
9 8 7 6 5 4 3 2 1

Library of Congress Cataloging-in-Publication Data

Vanderhoof, Gabrielle.
  Basketball / by Gabrielle Vanderhoof. — 1st ed.
      p. cm.
  Includes bibliographical references and index.
  ISBN 978-1-4222-1731-3   ISBN (set) 978-1-4222-1728-3
  1. Basketball—Juvenile literature. I. Title.
  GV885.1.V37 2010
  796.323—dc22
                                    2010007228

Produced by Harding House Publishing Service, Inc.
www.hardinghousepages.com
Interior Design by MK Bassett-Harvey.
Cover Design by Torque Advertising + Design.
Printed in the USA by Bang Printing.

Contents

SLAM DUNK
BASKETBALL

Introduction

GETTING THE EDGE: CONDITIONING, INJURIES, AND LEGAL & ILLICIT DRUGS is a fourteen-volume series written for young people who are interested in learning about various sports and how to participate in them safely. Each volume examines the history of the sport and the rules of play; it also acts as a guide for prevention and treatment of injuries, and includes instruction on stretching, warming up, and strength training, all of which can help players avoid the most common musculoskeletal injuries. Each volume also includes tips on healthy nutrition for athletes, as well as information on the risks of using performance-enhancing drugs or other illegal substances. GETTING THE EDGE offers ways for readers to healthily and legally improve their performance and gain more enjoyment from playing sports. Young athletes will find these volumes informative and helpful in their pursuit of excellence.

Sports medicine professionals assigned to a sport with which they are not familiar can also benefit from this series. For example, a football athletic trainer may need to provide medical care for a local gymnastics meet. Although the emergency medical principles and action plan would remain the same, the athletic trainer could provide better care for the gymnasts after reading a simple overview of the principles of gymnastics in GETTING THE EDGE.

Although these books offer an overview, they are not intended to be comprehensive in the recognition and management of sports injuries. They should not replace the professional advice of a trainer, doctor, or nutritionist. The text helps the reader appreciate and gain awareness of the sport's history, standard training techniques, common injuries, dietary guidelines, and the dangers of using drugs to gain an advantage. Reference material and directed readings are provided for those who want to delve further into these subjects.

Written in a direct and easily accessible style, GETTING THE EDGE is an enjoyable series that will help young people learn about sports and sports medicine.

—*Susan Saliba, Ph.D., National Athletic Trainers' Association Education Council*

1
Overview of Basketball

Understanding the Words

Professional has to do with activities that are done in order to earn a living; this means that the person doing them has to be skilled enough to be worth being paid well.

Someone who **persevered** kept going no matter what.

Offensive means "on the attack"; in basketball, the offensive team has the ball and is trying to make a basket.

Defensive means "withstanding attack"; in basketball, the defensive team does not have the ball and is protecting its basket.

In sports, **scouts** are people who look for talented younger players in order to sign them up for college or professional teams.

Competitive has to do with trying to win.

Rivalries are feelings of competition to see who is better.

SLAM DUNK
BASKETBALL

Basketball started as a simple game of a ball, ten players, two peach baskets, and a mere thirteen rules written on a single page. Today, the beloved sport has grown into a major industry and way of life for millions of people. However, the basics remain: the sport still utilizes skills such as dribbling and throwing to loop a ball through a hoop.

History of Basketball

During December of 1891, a Canadian physical educator named James Naismith wanted a sport to keep his students in shape during long New England winters. In the YMCA gymnasium at the International Training School in Springfield, Massachusetts, Naismith initially attempted indoor soccer and lacrosse. However, these sports simply could not be performed inside the confines of four walls; players ended up injured, and property was damaged. So Naismith decided to invent his own sport.

He wanted no roughhousing in his gym but a challenging sport that would use more skill than strength or speed. Ultimately, he nailed two peach baskets high on the walls of the gym. The first game was played with a soccer ball and nine students on each team (Naismith had eighteen students). A janitor was convinced to climb a ladder to retrieve the ball each time someone made a basket. Fortunately for the janitor, the first game ended with a score of 1–0. Eventually, the bottoms of the baskets were removed; the design was perfected when baskets were exchanged for wires, and a backboard was added.

The students immensely enjoyed the game and it was not long before the sport caught on in popularity among other schools and colleges. By 1897, teams of five were standardized. Basketball became an official Olympic sport in 1936 in Berlin, and a year later, it was the first national tournament hosted by the National Association of Intercollegiate Athletics (NAIA). In 1949, two **professional** leagues, the National Basketball League (formed in 1937) and the Basketball Association of America (formed in 1946) merged to form the National Basketball Association (NBA) that we know today. Currently, only eight of the original seventeen teams still remain, though only two of them still play in their original cities.

The name "basketball," is derived from the first time the game was played when real fruit baskets were attached to gym walls.

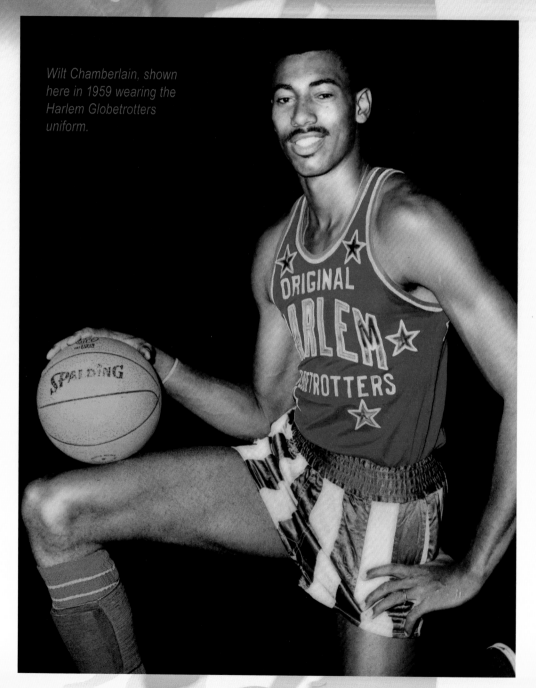

Wilt Chamberlain, shown here in 1959 wearing the Harlem Globetrotters uniform.

Wilt Chamberlain (1936-1999)

Remarkable player Wilt Chamberlain was inducted into the Naismith Basketball Hall of Fame in 1978.

Nicknamed "Wilt the Stilt" and the "Big Dipper," Wilt Chamberlain has been called the most awesome force ever seen on a basketball court. At 7 feet 1 inch (2.15 m) and 275 pounds (125 kg), he was unstoppable. He was the only NBA player to score 100 points in one game, and his other single-game records included eighteen straight field goals without a miss and fifty-five rebounds. He also held the NBA career record of 23,924 rebounds, was the second all-time scorer with 31,419 (behind Kareem Abdul-Jabbar), and was the only NBA player to score 4,000 points in one season.

Chamberlain played two years with the University of Kansas, and was named All-American both years. He then spent a season with the professional Harlem Globetrotters before becoming the NBA's Rookie of the Year in 1959 with the Philadelphia Warriors. In 1965, he joined the Philadelphia 76ers and was traded to the Los Angeles Lakers in 1968.

Retiring in 1973, Chamberlain had one other astonishing statistic: in 1,200 games, he never fouled out. He explained this with a smile: "They said I was too nice."

The Boston Celtics were the best team in the NBA from 1958–1966, winning eight championship titles in a row during these years. This image shows Bill Russell of the Celtics going up against Wilt Chamberlain of the Philadelphia 76ers in 1966.

By the 1950s, basketball had become a huge college sport, paving the way for professional basketball. By the 1960s, several pro teams all over the United States participated in competition. With the general public's growing interest due to players like Larry Bird and Magic Johnson, basketball went on to capture the hearts of Americans.

Several changes have been made since the early days of basketball. Early basketball players differed in appearance from today's players. Naismith's players wore wool jerseys with long sleeves and long pants, while today, players wear light jerseys with matching colors and individualized numbers for mobility and easy recognition. Originally, shots from the field had to be two-handed. If a player fouled, then anyone on the opposing team could shoot the free throws. Teams also could have any number of players (in 1892, Cornell University had fifty on each side) before the number was fixed at five. The original games were a lot rougher, often ending in fights and arguments. Wire cages were even constructed around the court to protect the audiences, and to prevent the audience from throwing bottles and other garbage onto the court. Some referees even carried guns as a means of controlling the games!

Women's basketball evolved a little differently. Women's uniforms were very constricting at first. The only body parts that weren't covered were fingers, necks, and heads. Otherwise, women were expected to wear floor-length

Women's basketball has been around nearly as long as men's basketball. The rules were first adapted for women in 1892, by Senda Berenson at Smith College. These women are the Smith College team from 1902.

necks, and heads. Otherwise, women were expected to wear floor-length dresses, petticoats, and slippers. Freedom came in 1896 when bloomers were introduced to women at Sophie Newcomb College in New Orleans. However, while women's basketball had just started to gain popularity, the nation was outraged to see well-bred women pulling hair, yelling, and shrieking. Parents, doctors, and physical education teachers were afraid to encourage girls to play in the sport. Women who did participate were encouraged to wear makeup for the games to help them look more dignified. However, as women **persevered** to win games and obtain TV ratings, women's basketball became more widely accepted, and by 2002, the Women's National Basketball Association (WNBA) drew in over two million viewers.

How to Play

The goal of basketball is to earn as many points as possible through shooting the ball through the hoops. The game is played on a rectangular court divided into equal halves by the mid-court line. The ball travels down the court through passing or dribbling. Members can gain possession of the ball through steals, contest shots, passes, and rebounds. The team controlling the ball is called the offense, while the other team is called the defense. When the **offensive** team puts the ball into play, they have ten seconds to get the ball out of their half of the court. Once they take the ball into the **defensive** side, they cannot backtrack into their own side. If either condition is not met, then the defensive team will be rewarded the ball.

Players can earn points several ways. They can make two-point goals by making a basket. A three-point goal is made if the shot comes from behind the three-point arc. Free throws after a foul earn only one point. A personal foul is made when a player has a misconduct: hitting, pushing, slapping, holding the ball, or illegal screening. Penalties also vary depending on the type of foul. During inbounds, players are fouled during play; their teams receive the ball

Basketball is played on a court that is divided into halves by what is called the mid-court line. Each half of the court has its own three-point arc, key, and basket.

and five seconds to pass it into the court from the nearest baseline. During a one-and-one, if a team has seven or more fouls, the player who was fouled is awarded a free throw. If he is successful, then he's rewarded another throw. In cases of ten or more fouls, the fouled player can receive two free throws.

Games are usually divided into two sessions. The tip-off determines which team receives the ball first. In college, each session is twenty minutes long, while in games played by younger players, the sessions are divided into eight- or six-minute quarters. During halftime, the two teams change sides. In pro games, quarters are twelve minutes long with several-minute breaks in between. If at the end of the game, both teams have the same score, then various periods of overtime are used until there's a clear winner.

Opportunities to Play Basketball

Because basketball requires so little equipment and only five players for a team, most young people are very familiar with the game at the neighborhood level. Good basketball teams can be sponsored by small schools that could never afford a football program, and by urban schools without the space for a stadium.

High school basketball is an ideal showcase for good players who wish to continue the sport at the college level, and many of these students apply for partial or full athletic scholarships. Star players will easily draw the attention of college **scouts**, and pro scouts will even court exceptional athletes. Several high school players have

High school and college basketball gives players a chance to build their skills and showcase their talents.

Lebron James (1984-)

A forward with the Cleveland Cavaliers, Lebron James was born in Akon, Ohio, where his single mother, Gloria James, raised him. He started playing basketball in elementary school. Then, he attended Saint-Vincent Mary High School where he became a varsity football player.

Once Lebron grew to 6 feet 7 inches in his sophomore year, he quit football to focus on a sport where he could use his height to his advantage. The summer before his junior year he played in the USA Basketball Developmental Festival in Colorado Springs, where he scored 120 points in five games, becoming MVP. Lebron was the first ever undergraduate to be invited to the tournament, and soon after was being compared to Magic Johnson.

In 2003, when he was only nineteen, his hometown team, the Cleveland Cavaliers, signed him on, and he landed an endorsement deal of $100 million. In 2009, a documentary was released about Lebron's life called **More Than a Game**. He was the first black man to appear on the cover of **Vogue Magazine**, and in 2007, he was ranked number one on the Forbes "Top Earners Under 25" list.

skipped college and gone directly into the professional game. Moses Malone, for example, signed with the Utah Stars of the American Basketball Association upon graduation from high school, as did Lebron James with the Cleveland Cavaliers of the National Basketball Association. Most players, however, seek the benefits of a college education— and enjoy the excitement of intercollegiate basketball.

There are other options for staying involved in basketball besides being a college or professional basketball player. Youth or high school level basketball is a great way to express your passion for the sport. The Amateur

Coaches can serve as great role models for kids and teens playing basketball, teaching sportsmanship and teamwork.

What People Say About Basketball

James Naismith, basketball inventor:
"The invention of basketball was not an accident. It was developed to meet a need. Those boys simply would not play 'Drop the Handkerchief.'"

Bill Vaughn, author:
"Any American boy can be a basketball star if he grows up, up, up."

Michael Jordan, former Chicago Bulls player:
"Every time I step onto the court, if you're against me, you're trying to take something from me. I don't want the other team to win. I just do not want them to win."

Bobby Knight, former Indiana University coach:
"You don't play against opponents. You play against the game of basketball."

Abe Lemons, Oklahoma City University coach:
"There are only two plays: Romeo and Juliet, and put the darn ball in the basket."

Tom Tolbert, Orlando Magic player:
"I look at the NBA as a football game without the helmet."

Types of Fouls

Basketball games are often won or lost from the free-throw line or because a good player fouls out. Illegal actions are divided into technical or personal fouls. A technical foul involves bad behavior that is usually not physical. Coaches may be charged for overreacting, such as running onto the court or yelling at an official. Players may be charged for touching an official, using obscenities, or complaining about a call.

Personal fouls include:

- Charging—The player with the ball collides with a defensive player whose feet are already firmly planted on the spot.
- Blocking—The defender's feet are not firmly planted before the ball carrier collides with him.
- Hand checking—A defender touches an offensive player facing her.
- Holding—A player grabs an opponent's uniform to hinder movement.
- Flagrant foul—An action so rough that it could result in injury.

Athletic Union, or AAU, is a nonprofit organization that sponsors individual clubs and allows teams to travel and compete against one another. Coaches organize teams within their community, which can be of any age or level.

High-school-level coaching is another great option. Because it can lead to careers in college basketball and the NBA, it is sometimes very **competitive**. **Rivalries** among schools, competitive parents, and college teams scouting for players are common and are what make the job challenging. The coach must work with the school, parents, and her team to ensure success. A great knowledge of the game is definitely a must, as well as the ability to motivate and inspire players.

While the players and head coach may be the only ones you notice during a college or professional basketball game, there are many individuals who work together to make the team a success. If you have a love for the sport, you can pursue a career in countless areas: sports journalist or commentator, team athletic trainer, assistant coaching job, and many others. If you are creative and look beyond the surface, you will find many opportunities. Talk to your own coach to get some ideas and advice on how he or she got started.

2
Mental Preparation

Understanding the Words

A **routine** *is when you do something the same way over and over; you make a habit of doing it exactly the same every time.*

To **visualize** *means to picture something in your mind.*

A **layup** *in basketball is usually a one-handed shot made close to the basket.*

How mentally prepared you are before a game is just as important as how ready you are physically; in fact, it might even be more important! It doesn't matter how many plays you've run through or the amount of free throws you've shot. If you're not confident and in a good state of mind, your performance will suffer.

Team discussion or meetings before and during games can help bolster a team's confidence and performance.

Visualizing success can often yield positive results, on and off the court. Having a positive attitude can make all the difference in a difficult game.

That's why it's vital to have a **routine** where you **visualize** positive details of a game before it even begins. With your imagination, you can create vivid pictures in your mind: jumping high to make a perfect shot, stealing the ball and going the length of the court for a **layup**, or standing at the foul line and making two shots that swish through the net. Think about the good plays you've made in previous games, and rehearse these in your mind, too, as if you were watching yourself on television.

Game Tactics

Basketball is a game that moves at such a fast pace you may wonder how it is possible to plan and carry out tactics. At college and professional levels, much time is spent in pregame preparation. Many hours are spent watching videos of opponents' earlier games to assess their offense and defense, and coaches will alter their team's strategy both before and during a game to take advantage of opponents' weaknesses. Other general strategies have also proven to work. Planning out these strategies ahead of time is an important part of the mental preparation for a basketball game.

Offense

- Screening play—A player stands between his teammate who has the ball and a defender. This action is called a "screen" or "pick." The player doing the screening is generally taller than the shooter.

- Fast break—Used by fast teams, this usually begins when a player rebounds an opponent's shot. Her teammates immediately sprint down court to receive her long pass over the defenders' heads.
- Give-and-go—One player passes the ball to a teammate and immediately cuts toward the basket to receive the ball back and shoot. This often works because the defender guarding the first player will relax when the ball is passed.

Defense

- Full-court press—Defensive players come right up to guard the opposing team that is throwing the ball into the play in the backcourt (which is the farthest away from the offense's own basket). This can disrupt the offense and even lead to interceptions of the throw-in.
- Intentional fouling—A team behind at a late stage of the game will often foul an offensive player just to stop the clock. It is best to foul a player with the ball who has a poor record making free shots.
- Time-out—In strategic terms, a time-out enables a team to break the momentum of an opponent on a successful run. A full 75-second time-out is sometimes just enough to cool down a hot offense.

People Who Used Visualization to Succeed

"When I'm about to fall asleep, I visualize to the point that I know exactly what I want to do: dive, glide, stroke, flip, reach the wall, hit the split time to the hundredth, then swim back again for as many times as I need to finish the race."
—Michael Phelps, 14-time Olympic swimming champion

"When I was very young I visualized myself being and having what it was I wanted. Mentally I never had any doubts about it. The mind is really so incredible."
—Arnold Schwarzenegger, 5-time Mr. Universe, actor, politician

Steven Balzac, a former professional athlete, has used this technique throughout his career. "If we imagine success, we prepare ourselves for success because that's what's in our heads," he says. "What you imagine is what you get." Even if you are a younger athlete or one that hasn't had too much experience, this technique will come in handy. Again, take advice from Balzac: "When I was a competitive fencer, I would watch the really accomplished guys fencing and imagine what they were doing. I would then shift the image of them doing it to me doing it."

The key to visualization is to make the image as realistic as possible. Imagine you're in the heat of the moment, the clock is ticking down, the crowd is cheering, and your coach is yelling. The better you can mentally handle the stress, the better you will be when it comes time to perform in real life. Imagine the entire atmosphere: the sounds of squeaking shoes, the smack of the ball on the floor, the referee's whistle, your own breathing—and then picture making the final shot as the buzzer sounds.

Visualization must be practiced regularly and become an important part of your preparation. Do it before a practice or game, or even while taking a bath or before falling asleep. The more often you "see" yourself making great plays, the more likely it will seem. This visualization is important in order to create a positive self-image for yourself, increase confidence, and reduce anxiety and injuries.

Relaxed attention is another common practice among athletes. It means controlling your thoughts, emotions, and tension while playing. Notice how many basketball players become focused and calm when waiting for another player's

Focus and calm determination is more useful than anxiety, worry, or panic when playing sports.

Michael Jordan is known as one of the greatest basketball players of all time. He is best known for his years with the Chicago Bulls, from 1984–1993, and after a brief retirement to play baseball, from 1995–1998.

Michael Jordan (1963-)

Michael Jordan is considered to be one of the best basketball players ever. From the mid-1980s to the late 1990s, he dominated the world of basketball, leading the Chicago Bulls to six national championships, while earning the National Basketball Association's (NBA) Most Valuable Player Award five times.

Michael's father said his son was competitive from the time he was young. He wanted to win every game he played. "What he does have is a competition problem. He was born with that. . . . The person he tries to outdo most of the time is himself."

Michael went to college at the University of North Carolina at Chapel Hill in 1981, and he soon became an important member of the school's basketball team. His team won the NCAA Division I championships in 1982, with Michael scoring the final basket needed to defeat Georgetown University. In 1983 and in 1984, he received the NCAA College Player of the Year. During the summer of 1984, Michael went to the Olympics as a member of the U.S. basketball team, which won the gold at the games held in Los Angeles. (Eight years later, Michael Jordan also helped the United States bring home the gold at the 1992 Olympic Games held in Barcelona, Spain.)

Michael left college after his junior year to join the Chicago Bulls. He helped the team make it to the play-offs and scored an average of 28.2 points per game that season. He received the NBA Rookie of the Year Award and was selected for the All-Star Game.

In 1985, he finished his bachelor's degree in geography and continued to play basketball professionally. He became the first player since Wilt Chamberlin to score more than 3,000 points in a single season. By the late 1980s, the Chicago Bulls was a rising team, and Michael played a major role in the team's success. Michael Jordan became known for his power and agility on the court as well as for his leadership abilities. He gained even more attention when he landed several endorsement deals with companies such as Nike.

In 1992, the Chicago Bulls won their second NBA championship title. The team was at the top of the basketball world, and they took their third championship the following year. Michael, however, had a personal tragedy: his father was shot during a robbery. With his world shaken, Michael Jordan made a decision that shocked the sports world: he decided to retire from basketball to play baseball. He played for a minor league team, the Birmingham Barons, as an outfielder for a year.

foul shot. They are practicing relaxed attention. Despite the energy required for a game, a player who controls anxiety and anger can avoid mistakes. The team with the most confident and relaxed attitude is most apt to win a close basketball game between equal teams. Mental conditioning backs up physical training, and this is a winning combination on the basketball court.

A common routine that professional athletes often follow is meditation. If you are stressed and nervous before a big game, for example, take a few minutes to mentally remove yourself from the high-energy atmosphere to decrease your jitters. By closing your eyes, breathing deeply, and quieting your thoughts, you will gain many benefits that will help you play. Meditation decreases heart rate and increases blood flow, reduces anxiety and muscle tension, and increases self-confidence.

Another mental practice that's been a part of basketball for years is superstition.

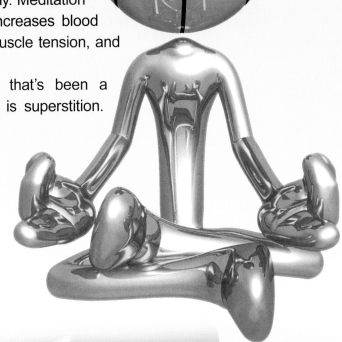

Some professional basketball players choose to meditate before games to clear their minds of anxiety and negativity.

Common in almost every sport, superstitious acts are individual to each athlete and help them feel more prepared for a game. Most of these routines seem silly—but they can help build a player's sense of confidence. For example, Michael Jordan of the Chicago Bulls always wore the same pair of shorts during games, and many players have a "lucky" item of clothing. Some players wear the same pair of socks every game, without washing them, until

Some players have superstitions about the equipment they use, the clothes they wear, or the things they do before and during a game. A player may wear the same shoes for every game, for instance.

the team loses. According to basketball tradition, the last person to make a basket during warm-up will have a good game. Generally, each player has a specific "lucky" pattern of dribbling the ball before making a foul shot. It doesn't matter whether these superstitions have anything to do with good luck or not, so long as they help the athlete to be more confident.

3
Physical Preparation

Understanding the Words

Your respiratory system *is made up of the parts of your body, including your lungs, that take in oxygen and release carbon dioxide.*

Stamina *means the power to keep going.*

Calisthenics *are exercises designed to develop muscular tone and promote physical well-being.*

Cartilage *is the firm, rubbery tissue that cushions bones at joints; a more flexible kind of cartilage connects muscles with bones and makes up other parts of the body, such as the larynx and the outside parts of the ears.*

When referring to your muscles, your core *has to do with the stomach, back, and hips.*

Your abdominals *are the muscles in your lower stomach.*

Your obliques *are the part of your abdominal muscles that allow you to twist and turn your trunk.*

Your back extensors *are the muscles that allow you to bend and straighten your back.*

Cardiovascular *has to do with your heart and blood vessels. (Cardio = heart, vascular = vessels.)*

Aerobic *has to do with exercises that depend on increased oxygen consumption; these exercises help strengthen your lungs and heart.*

Anaerobic *has to do with exercises that increase muscle strength; these exercises use oxygen more quickly than the body is able to replenish it inside the working muscle, and as a result, muscle fibers have to get their energy from stored sources.*

Weight training *is an example of anaerobic exercise.*

Metabolic *has to do with the biochemical processes that are necessary for life.*

Lateral *means sideways.*

Basketball has always been a contact sport, but stronger and more aggressive players have made the game much more physical (although luckily not dangerous enough to bring back cages!). The possibility of injury is always present, so pregame warm-ups and long-term conditioning programs are essential.

The warm-up session before each game is a good rehearsal of basketball skills. Watching a warm-up, you will notice that players often begin very leisurely: stretching their arms, bouncing the ball, passing it around a circle of players, and taking several unhurried shots at the basket. The tempo then quickens, as players pass the ball to loosen their arms and help hand-eye coordination. They also practice rebounding, and line up to make running layups. All this involves the key abilities demanded by basketball: accuracy, teamwork, and bursts of energy.

Such moderate exercise also prepares a player's body for the considerable demands that this fast game makes on muscles and the **respiratory system**. Basketball does not have football's routine breaks in action or baseball's half-inning rests. If no fouls occur, basketball players must have the **stamina** to race back and forth on the court for long periods of time without a pause.

Warm-Up and Preconditioning

A pregame workout of even fifteen minutes will stretch and warm the muscles, ligaments, and connective tissues, making them supple so that a player's body is more flexible. Stretching should start with the neck and work downward to the shoulders, back, and legs. This "loosening up" will cut down on injuries on the court that might have been caused by stiffness, such as muscle strains, pulls, or tears. These exercises will also add more oxygen to your body's system by increasing the heart and respiratory rates. Any exercise that provides an increased oxygen intake is called aerobic and will produce positive benefits less than a minute after the exercise begins.

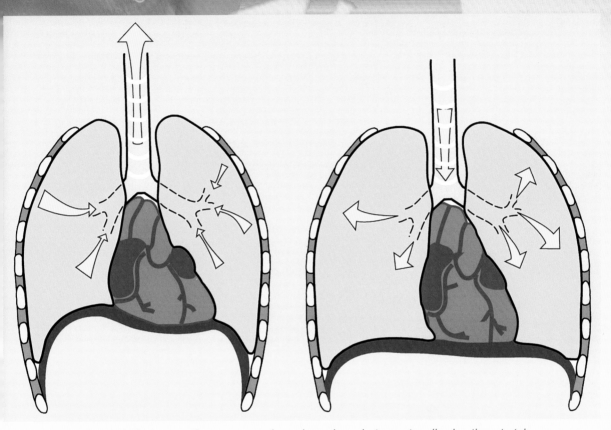

Warming up before a practice or game raises players' respiratory rate, allowing them to take more oxygen into their bodies.

Although basketball players do pregame stretching exercises on the court, they will not use the hard floor to engage in basic **calisthenics** such as sit-ups, push-ups, running in place, jumping jacks, and knee bends, as seen before football games. If they want to do such additional stretching and strength movements, they will use the locker room for these.

After a game has ended, players should cool down for two to five minutes to help slow the heart and breathing to their normal tempo. The strenuous play on the basketball court makes a player's heart to work hard to pump blood to the muscles, and blood that remains in the muscles causes a sore or stiff feeling after the game. Walking or stretching will relieve this feeling, but sitting down immediately afterwards could cause dizziness or fainting.

It's also important to stay fit not only during the season, but throughout the year. Aerobic and strength conditioning are the best ways to build up insurance against fatigue, which has been proven to cause injuries on the court. Any combination of running, swimming, cycling, and warm-up exercises will be beneficial. A player's endurance and general good health will be improved by strenuous exercise lasting from twenty to thirty minutes three or more days a week. Too much physical training, however, can cause exhaustion, stress, and poor performance. Young players who aren't fully grown should not do heavy **weight training**, as this may damage the body's **cartilage**, causing stunted growth.

Exercising to Be Flexible

Upper body warm-up exercises concentrate on the neck, arms, shoulders, waist, and back. Here are few good ones:

- Stretch the neck by grabbing the back of the head with the right hand and pulling the head to the right. Repeat with the left hand.
- Stretch the arms upward and backward.
- Reach the arms toward the sky one at a time.
- Rotate the arms forward in circles on either side, moving one up as the other descends.
- Hold each elbow behind the head in a pulling motion.
- Raise arms to shoulder level, pulling them back and holding the position.

- Raise the shoulders while keeping the arms next to the body, and then move the shoulders backward in slow circles and then forward.

- For the waist, hold the arms out to the side and swing them as you twist your body back and forth to the right and left.

- For the back, lie on your front with your legs crossed at the ankles and your arms straight out in front. Raise your upper body off the floor five times, holding each time for one second, and then slowly lower it back to the floor.

Stretching before any athletic activity is important to loosen and warm up muscles and joints. Basketball players need to spend extra time stretching their arms and shoulders, since these will be used a lot during a practice or game.

Flexibility exercises for the lower body are extremely important in basketball. These are usually done either sitting or lying down. Here is a collection of stretches for the muscles from the lower back to the toes:

- Pointed toes: Walk on your heels with your feet flexed—toes pointed—to keep your shin muscles tightened. Walk about 10 yards, 4 times.

- Side lunge: To stretch your hamstring and thighs, stand in a straddle position facing forward. Slowly lean to your right while keeping your back straight and your feet at 45 degrees. Keep your left knee from moving past your right foot and point the toes of your left foot upwards. Hold this position for 15 seconds, then switch legs and repeat twice.

- Lying crossover: Lie on your back with both legs extended to one side. Lift your right leg and cross it over your body, resting it close to your left hand, keeping your shoulders flat on the ground. Hold for 10–15 seconds, and then switch sides. This stretches the buttocks, lower spine, and oblique muscles.

- Groin stretch: Sit down with your knees bent, facing outward and the bottom of your feet touching one another. Slowly stretch your legs, pressing your knees as close to the ground as you can, then hold for 15 seconds. Repeat.

Training

Equally as important as stretching and conditioning are all types of training, both during the season and off-season. The most common types include weight training, resistance training, plyometrics, and cardio training.

Conditioning Tips

- Before any exercise session, always remember first to do a light warm-up and to stretch.
- Begin your conditioning program by exercising lightly, from thirty minutes to an hour, depending on your fitness level. Slowly increase the time each day. It will take from six to eight weeks to reach top condition.
- Do not exercise or practice basketball for more than ninety minutes each session. The key to conditioning is physical intensity and concentration, not longer workouts.
- Select exercises for flexibility and strength, and add relaxation techniques that were discussed in chapter 2.
- Exercise to the full capacity of your body's limits, but never endanger your health or safety by going beyond them.

Weight Training

This is done with weights and resistance machines in order to develop and define the muscles. It helps build stamina and strength and also helps to prevent injuries.

First and foremost, the emphasis should be on lower body strength—hips and legs—as this is what powers you most on the court. Next, concentrate on core strength, including abdominals, obliques, and back extensors. Lastly, be sure to include upper body weight training to develop the arm and back muscles.

Here is a sample weight lifting routine, ideal for basketball players during the off-season, when the hardest and most intense lifting should be done. Perform this routine 2 -3 times a week:

- Squats: four sets of 15, 12, and 10 repetitions
- Lunges: three sets of 15, 12, and 10 repetitions
- Bench Press: four sets of 15, 12, and 10 repetitions
- Shoulder Press and Arm Curls: four sets of 5, 12, and 10 repetitions.
- Core Training: sit-ups, leg lifts, and exercises using a medicine ball will give the best resistance.

Weight training, such as the bench press, can be an excellent way to increase muscle strength, but younger athletes should check with a doctor first to learn what will be safe for them.

Plyometrics, commonly referred to as "plyos" in sports lingo, are a very important part of your basketball training. Plyometrics are exercise drills that involve movements like jumping, hopping, sprinting, or quick movements for the upper body. These actions train the body how to jump higher, faster, and react quicker. They are designed to increase balance, coordination, quickness, and overall bodily power. Through muscle memory, the nervous system will allow the body to know how to automatically react on the court and during a game. Plyometric exercises work on improving a player's strength, power, flexibility, conditioning, and overall skill level.

- "The Skier" is an exercise that works to quicken foot speed and improve overall explosiveness and physical condition. You can perform it on the court or any stable surface. Bend your knees as if you are skiing and jump from one side to the other, making it look as if your feet barely touch the ground or as though you are landing on a hot surface. Start with two sets and perform both within thirty seconds. As your stamina and skills increase, also increase the duration of each drill.

- Left Foot/Right Foot Touches also aim to improve foot speed and overall condition. Start with two sets per foot, lasting for about twenty-five seconds each, with a rest period lasting the same amount of time. Position the left foot on the ground, and your right foot in front of you, not touching the ground. The left foot moves forward while the right swings backward, moving like a pendulum. Next, swing the right foot back, making sure it doesn't touch the ground while the opposite leg goes forward, switching positions. The foot that touches the ground should move back and forth about 10 inches as quickly as possible, while the other leg will help balance the body and keep you upright. As your fitness increases, add about five seconds to this exercise every two weeks, finishing at about fifty-five seconds per leg. Remember, however long you do the exercise, you should also rest for the same period of time.

Although plyometrics are vital parts of training, they should never be overdone. In fact, basketball is a plyometrics workout in itself, so adding plyometric exercises on top of a too-tough training schedule can be more dangerous than helpful.

The final piece to the puzzle in keeping fit for basketball is **cardiovascular** training, or cardio for short. If you have the skills to outsmart the other team's players, they will do no good if you can't keep up with them throughout the game. It's important to be in top physical condition once basketball season rolls around, and endurance is a huge part of this.

First, a good **aerobic** workout routine is key. You should establish a routine that consists of thirty to forty-five minutes of activity three to four days a week. The most common cardio activity for athletes is running, but there are many options.

- Exercise bike: 30–45 minutes

- Jogging: 30 minutes

- Elliptical machine: 30 minutes

- Aerobics class: 30 minutes

- Water exercise: 30 minutes

These are just a few suggestions, but it is important to mix up your workouts for many reasons. For example, while running is very effective, it can become stressful on the body if it is done for long periods. You are at a higher risk of injury if you only take part in one activity as opposed to a variety, and by being creative with your workouts, they will not feel as boring and monotonous.

Target Heart Rate

You should know your Maximum Heart Rate and your correct training zone to know if you are training at the right pace. Here are a few ways to figure your target heart rate. You can find your Target Heart Rate (thr) with this method: subtract your age from 220 (226 for women). Find your training zone below and multiply that number times your maximum rate.

Training Zones

Healthy Heart Zone (warm up): 50–60% of maximum heart rate.

Aerobic Zone (endurance training): 70–80% of maximum heart rate. The aerobic zone will improve your cardiovascular and respiratory system, and increase the size and strength of your heart. This is the preferred zone if you are training for endurance.

Anaerobic Zone (performance training): 80–90% of maximum heart rate. This high-intensity training will help you fight fatigue better.

Red Line (maximum effort): 90–100% of maximum heart rate. You should only train in this zone if you are in very good shape and have been cleared by a physician to do so.

Interval training is the second part of a solid cardio workout, and includes **anaerobic** activity, timed recovery periods following brief but intense runs. The goal of interval training is to condition your body to become accustomed to the high-intensity running and the brief time-outs that often follow that are very specific to basketball (for instance, while another player is making a foul shot, and you are watching, trying to catch your breath). These anaerobic sessions should range from a 1:1 to a 1:3 work/rest ratio, in order to best imitate activity during an actual game. (In other words, if you exercise for ten minutes, you should rest for 10 to 30 minutes.) Including sprints from 800 meters down to 10 meters will ensure solid preparation.

Stretching thoroughly before starting any activity, especially interval training, is vital. In addition to your general warm-up and stretching, you should also include a sprint-specific warm-up to ready your muscles for anaerobic workouts.

The final stage of a cardio workout should be basketball-specific **metabolic** training. This preparation includes metabolic conditioning as well as basketball drills. Here is a detailed example:

- Start on the baseline, sprint to the free-throw line and back
- Immediately sprint to the opposite baseline and back
- Immediately spring to half-court and backpedal back
- Rest 25 seconds
- **Lateral** slide to free throw (left arm lead) and slide back
- Sprint to half-court and backpedal back

DID YOU KNOW?

The easiest place to feel your own heartbeat is the carotid artery. Place your index finger on the side of your neck between the middle of your collar bone and your jawline. (You can also use the artery on the underside of your wrist.) You can count the beats for a full 60 seconds—or count for 6 seconds and add a zero at the end. In other words, if you felt your heartbeat 14 times in 6 seconds, your heart rate would be 140.

- Lateral slide to free-throw line (right arm lead) and slide back
- Rest 25 seconds
- Repeat this drill for a total of six repetitions, changing the commands each time.

This basketball player is doing a running workout sometimes known as a "suicide run," which involves sprinting quickly back-and-forth between lines on the court, stopping to touch each line before turning and sprinting back to the first. The quick stop-and-start nature of this workout is an excellent way to get your body fit for a real game.

Larry Bird (1956-)

As a teenager, Larry Bird played guard during his sophomore and junior years, but he did not truly excel at basketball until his senior year. During his senior year he averaged 30.6 points and 20 rebounds per game, and colleges around the country began scouting him.

Larry initially decided to play for Indiana University, but he felt overwhelmed by the size of the campus and left after only a few weeks. He went back home, and though he finally decided to attend Indiana State University, he had to sit out the first season. He began his college playing career with the Sycamores in 1976 and was soon a national collegiate star.

In 1979, Larry signed with the Boston Celtics for $3,250,000 over five years; at the time, this was the largest rookie contract in NBA history. During his years with the Celtics, Larry grew to become one of the greatest talents in the NBA. He led Boston to three NBA championships, won numerous MVP awards, and is credited with again making the Celtics a formidable franchise.

In 1992, plagued by back problems, Larry Bird retired and accepted the position of special assistant in the Celtics front office for five seasons. In 1997, he became head coach of the

Indiana Pacers, and a year later he was named NBA Coach of the Year after leading the Pacers to a 58–24 season, the best in franchise history. That same year he was elected to the Basketball Hall of Fame. In 2000, he lead the Pacers to the NBA finals, but he stood by his previous decision to retire. Three years later, in 2003, Larry Bird joined the Pacers as president of basketball operations.

Follow this by a two-minute rest period while shooting free throws, and repeat the drill. Depending on your current conditioning level, you can adjust the amount of repetitions, but always aim for the maximum amount you feel you can do without pushing yourself too hard, which can lead to injury.

While all of this exercise is very important to getting and staying fit for basketball season, it's vital that you practice under the supervision of a coach or a personal trainer. If you perform these exercises without the right techniques, you can do your body more harm than good. The first few times that you do weight lifting in the gym, you should have one-on-one instruction on how to handle the weights, and you should never lift alone.

4
Common Injuries, Treatment, & Recovery

Understanding the Words

Acute *means very serious, with a sudden onset.*

Chronic *describes a condition that is long-lasting or recurs frequently.*

Your **Achilles tendon** *is the large tendon that runs from your heel to your calf.*

Your **quadriceps** *is the large muscle in your thigh that extends your leg.*

A **concussion** *is an injury to the brain as a result of a violent blow, shaking, or spinning. A concussion can cause immediate and usually temporary impairment of brain function such as thinking, vision, balance, and consciousness.*

A survey by the U.S. Consumer Product Safety Commission for kids age five to fourteen found that basketball, surprisingly, led all sports in the annual number of injuries: 574,000 incidents a year, more than double those of baseball and over 100,000 more than football.

There are very few protective items for basketball players, but the ones that are available can reduce injuries. Mouth guards will protect the mouth and teeth, and safety glasses should replace regular glasses. Knee and elbow pads, while they aren't regularly used, offer good protection from bruises and scrapes that occur on the court, and ankle supports can be worn to reduce the chance of ankle sprains. But the best equipment to prevent injuries is a good pair of basketball shoes. They should have solid support, fit snugly, and have good traction so you don't skid. This can reduce ankle sprains, knee injuries, low

More injuries occur in basketball than in any other sport, at 574,000 per year. A good pair of basketball shoes can prevent many injuries that are common in basketball.

back pain, and many other discomforts. Also, shoes that are not the right size, or that have poor support around the feet and ankles, can cause blisters.

There are many factors important to safety that are not always in the hands of the players, particularly the condition of the court. The backboard and all supporting bars must be adequately padded, and the walls behind the baskets should be padded as well and never too close to the baskets. The officials' table should not be near the boundary lines, bleachers, or other structures. The floor must be clean, without debris, and definitely not slippery. If a game is played outside, it is very important to check for natural hazards, such as holes and rocks. Night games should be properly lit.

Types of Injuries

During a game, players should be alert to the danger of collisions, keeping an eye on other players' movements. Another way of reducing injuries is to play fair, refraining from tripping, pushing, holding, elbowing, blocking, or charging into opponents. Even if players do their best to avoid these fouls, however, the generally rough nature of the game often leads to various types of injury due to collisions or falls.

ACUTE OR ACUTE TRAUMATIC INJURIES

This can be caused by a bad fall or any hard hit during a game, such as a collision with another player. **Acute** injuries include contusions, abrasions, lacerations, sprains, strains, and fractures. "Contusion" is the medical name for a bruise, which may be bad enough to cause swelling and bleeding in the muscles or other tissues. An abrasion is a scrape, and a laceration is a cut that is usually deep enough to require stitches. A sprain is a stretch or tear of a ligament, which is the tissue that supports joints by connecting bones and cartilage. If a stretch or tear occurs in a muscle or tendon (the tissue that connects muscles to bones), this is a strain. A fracture involves a crack, break, or shattering of a bone.

OVERUSE OR CHRONIC INJURIES

This kind of injury is caused by repeating the same action many times, as when a center rebounds the ball over and over until she experiences an ache in her ankles or knees. This is not as serious as an acute injury, but any **chronic** problem may become worse during the season, so players should seek medical advice and treatment.

Common Injuries

Basketball requires the active use of the whole body. The lower part is injured most often, but the upper body, including the head, can sustain injuries, particularly in a hard fall.

ANKLE AND FOOT INJURIES

Because basketball is a game of running and jumping, it places great demands on your feet and ankles. The most common plays, such as quickly cutting around a defensive player or leaping high for a rebound, may result in an uncertain landing, subjecting ankles and feet to continuous stress. Young players put additional wear and tear on these parts when they play on outdoor concrete courts. The strenuous action on any court can result in ankle sprains, heel bruises, and fractures. A sprain that severely stretches the ligaments of the outside ankle is fairly common in basketball because players make rapid changes in direction.

You will feel immediate pain and sometimes hear a crack when a tear occurs. Swelling will follow any sprain, and a trainer or coach will apply ice to the ankle when the player returns to the bench. As soon as possible, begin a treatment program known as R.I.C.E., which stands for Rest, Ice, Compression, and Elevation. Put the ice in a plastic bag, lay a towel on the injured ankle, and put the ice on the towel. Never place ice directly on the injured area. Do this for about twenty minutes at a time and repeat every two hours. Compression involves applying pressure to the ankle with an elastic bandage, making sure it

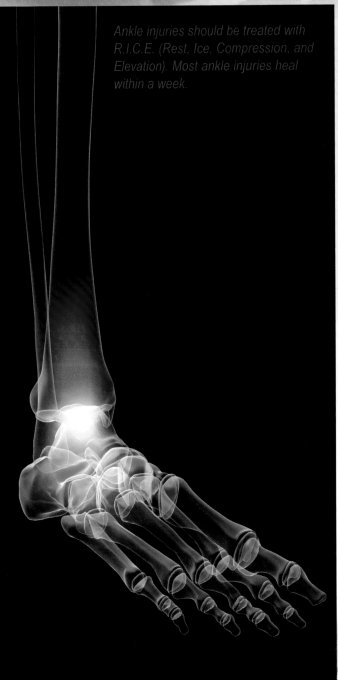

Ankle injuries should be treated with R.I.C.E. (Rest, Ice, Compression, and Elevation). Most ankle injuries heal within a week.

is not tight enough to restrict blood flow. Finally, elevate the ankle above heart level as much as possible. To improve support and prevent a recurrence of the injury, tape the ankle or use an ankle brace. A mild sprain should heal in about a week; severe ones can take up to six weeks.

A heel bruise can happen when a player leaps for the ball and lands incorrectly on the base of his heel instead of his toes. Poorly fitting shoes may also bruise the heels where the **Achilles tendon** attaches the back of the heel to the muscles of the calf of the leg. Achilles tendonitis, in which the tendon becomes inflamed, is a common injury. To treat heel bruises, follow the R.I.C.E. program and wear a doughnut-shaped felt pad on the bruised area.

A fracture to a foot bone is common when a player falls

Rehabilitation (Rehab)

The recovery period after an injury may take several weeks or even months. Once the pain has subsided, you might feel completely fit, but follow your doctor's advice about changes to your athletic activity or even time away from the game. Such injuries as sprained ankles and dislocated shoulders can quickly return if you reenter competition too soon. And even after rehabilitation, an injured area may begin to hurt again during a game. If so, stop immediately and tell your doctor.

Depending on how badly you are injured, your road back to fitness may include physical therapy or ultrasound to the injured area. Because injuries will cause you to lose muscle strength, rehabilitation will also include an exercise program. (If, for example, you wear a cast on your arm or leg for about six weeks, you may lose up to 40 percent of the strength you had in that arm or leg before the injury.) Recommended exercises may include swimming or workouts on gym equipment, such as a rowing machine.

or when another competitor lands on her foot, especially during rebounds. A bone can also develop tiny cracks from overuse, such as the running and leaping required by the game, and this is called a stress fracture. Any fracture may hurt and cause a limp. The injured player should see a physician, who will take an X-ray. To heal a fracture, rest is particularly important, so follow the R.I.C.E. method and use a brace.

CARTILAGE INJURIES

Cartilage injuries can happen when a player has a leg firmly on the court and the knee is twisted hard. The cartilage breaks off from the knee bone, causing swelling and pain. The knee will develop stiffness and popping sensations, and it might be difficult to extend the leg because of the knee locking. Players who are still growing are more likely to suffer this injury; about one-third of these injuries will heal with rest, although it may also be necessary to wear a cast for several weeks. Usually, surgery is required in older teens and adults.

A hard blow, such as falling on the court, can cause a dislocated kneecap. This movable bone at the front of the knee (also called

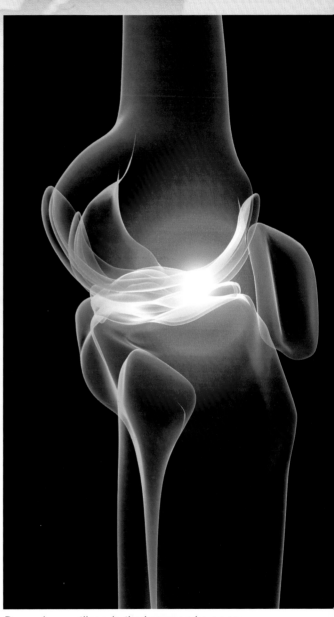

Damaging cartilage in the knee can be a very serious injury, sometimes requiring surgery.

the patella) is pushed sideways, causing swelling and severe pain. A bulge can develop on the side of the knee, and walking may be affected. The R.I.C.E. treatment may help, but the kneecap may have to be reset by a physician, and the player may need to wear a brace to prevent a recurrence of the injury.

Tendonitis of the knee is an inflammation of the tendon that connects the kneecap to the thighbone. Sometimes called "jumper's knee," this overuse injury is caused by running and jumping, which stretches the tendon. The swelling can make bending the knee, trying to lift and extend the leg, or even simple walking very painful. Again, R.I.C.E. is the best treatment.

LEG

Injuries to the leg are a fact of life in basketball. Players use their legs to jockey for positions or to block the progress of the ball, which can lead injuries. These injuries range from common contusions to hamstring pulls; infrequent fractures are generally caused by falls. A leg contusion, or bruise, is a common injury, especially in the **quadriceps**. The soreness can be reduced by ice packs, and the bruise will soon go away. Deeper bruises, however, rupture blood vessels in the area, and this blood can collect and cause serious problems if the muscle continues to be exercised. The most important part of the R.I.C.E. program for this injury is to elevate the leg to reduce blood "pooling," or collecting in one place. A physician should also always be consulted in the case of deep bruises.

Hamstring pulls (strains or tears) involve the large muscles at the back of the thigh and are usually caused by running and jumping. The muscle fibers are strained when a player runs fast, then suddenly changes the motion of her thigh, from being pulled forward by the quadriceps to being pulled backward by the hamstrings. To treat, use R.I.C.E. along with stretching exercises, and take about a four-week rest from playing.

Fractures occur rarely in basketball, but broken legs (and arms) may result from a severe fall or violent collision with another player. More common are stress fractures due to overuse. Both types of fracture occur most often in the tibia (the larger leg bone below the knee) and fibula (the outer, thinner leg bone below the knee). Male players have more fractures of the tibia, and females have more of the fibula. A physician will take X-rays and then, depending on the seriousness of the injury, fit splints or recommend that the player use crutches.

HANDS, WRISTS, AND FINGERS

Injuries to these areas occur while receiving passes, shooting, rebounding, and while breaking falls. Wrists are commonly sprained when the hand is bent too

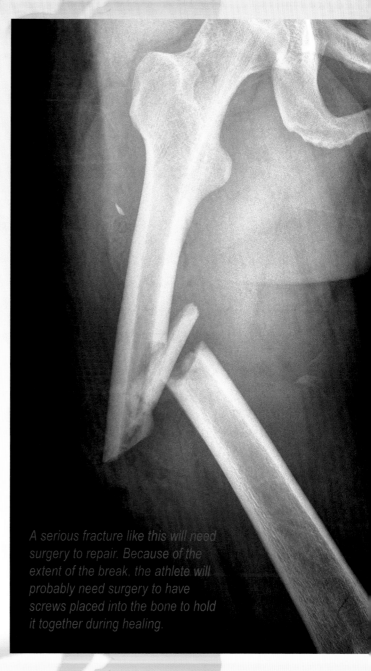

A serious fracture like this will need surgery to repair. Because of the extent of the break, the athlete will probably need surgery to have screws placed into the bone to hold it together during healing.

far forward or backward. The thumb and other fingers can be sprained, dislocated, jammed, or fractured when catching the ball or falling. Players can also develop stress fractures in all of these bones. If the pain does not go away within twenty-four hours, consult a doctor. X-rays are needed, and treatment includes ice, and in the case of fractures, a splint.

SHOULDERS

Shoulders can be injured by overuse, which causes strain, inflammation, or tendonitis. More severe are the two main injuries caused by falls and collisions: a shoulder separation or a dislocation.

The separation of a shoulder involves a ligament tear that causes the collarbone to move upward. This is normally corrected by rest and strengthening exercises. A rehabilitation period is usually required before a player can return to the court.

A dislocated shoulder occurs when the head of the humerus (upper arm bone) pops out of its socket. This requires immediate treatment. A torn cartilage or loose ligaments generally cause the dislocation. X-rays will be taken, and a shoulder sling should be worn for about three weeks. The most serious dislocations require surgery.

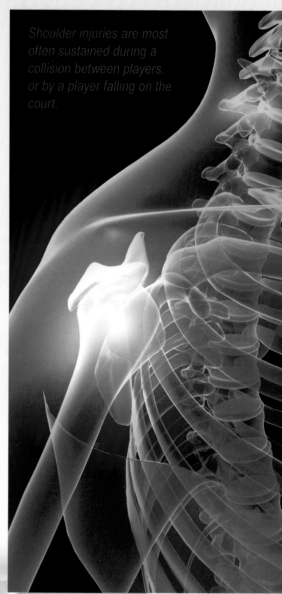

Shoulder injuries are most often sustained during a collision between players, or by a player falling on the court.

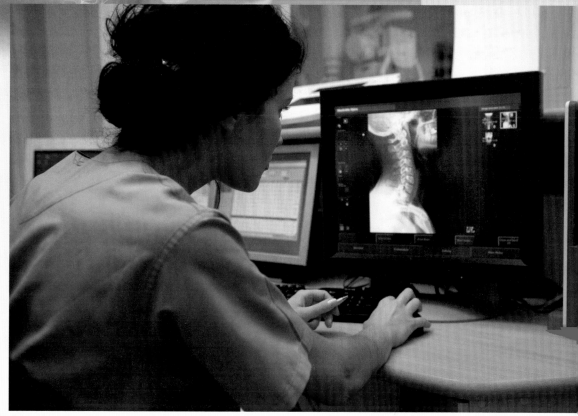

If a player sustains a neck injury, he will likely need to get an X-ray before the full extent of his injury is understood.

NECK

Serious neck injuries are rare in basketball. A more frequent problem is a "stinger" injury, which occurs when the nerves of the neck are overstretched, causing stinging pain and a temporary numbness. Punched nerves, which can be caused by a quick sideways twist of the neck, produce a burning pain in both the neck and often down the arm. The standard treatment is once again the R.I.C.E. program. Minor neck injuries, including bruises and sprains, may require that the player wear a neck collar or brace. Much

Kobe Bryant (1978-)

It's no wonder Kobe Bryant grew up to be a basketball star: his father was former NBA star, Joe "Jellybean" Bryant who played for the 76ers, Clippers, and Rockets. When Kobe was six years old, Joe Bryant started playing basketball in Europe, so the family moved to Italy, where they stayed for seven years. Kobe Bryant learned to speak fluent Italian—and he started playing basketball.

His family moved back to the United States when Kobe was 13, and he started playing high school basketball in Philadelphia. Kobe was now 6'6" and a star on the court. In his senior year of high school, he led his school to the Pennsylvania State Championship and was named the Naismith Player of the Year.

Kobe skipped college and was drafted right after high school by the Charlotte Hornets in the first round of the 1996 NBA draft. Then, in a trade the Hornets are still sorry they made, they sent Kobe to the LA Lakers. He played in the NBA All-Star Game for the first time in 1998, and by 2000, he had developed into one of basketball's best players. Kobe and Shaquille O'Neal teamed up to lead the LA Lakers to three straight NBA Championship Titles from 2000 to 2002. In 2008, Kobe won his first MVP award that year, and he continues to be a basketball superstar.

more dangerous is a fracture to the spine, or the vertebrae and discs can be compressed by a hard fall on the court when the head is bent forward. This injury is very rare, but a player lying still on the court should not be moved until qualified emergency personnel arrive; movement could cause paralysis or death. X-rays will reveal the extent of the injury.

HEAD

Severe falls during play may also result in a **concussion**. This injury is normally mild, causing a headache, poor balance, a lack of alertness, memory loss, and sometimes unconsciousness. There is a very rare chance that such a blow can cause pressure and a hematoma (bleeding under the skull), which can be fatal. For this reason, a physician will order X-rays and scans to eliminate such a possibility. Any head injury will require a player to wait for at least a week, even a month, after the symptoms disappear before returning to competition.

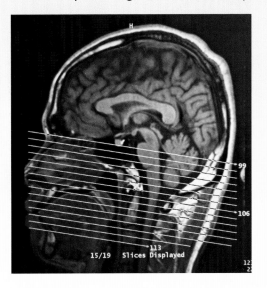

Some players who sustain head injuries may need to undergo what is called an MRI (a scan of the head and brain) in order for doctors to know what, if any, major damage has been done to the brain.

5
Nutrition & Dietary Supplements

Understanding the Words

A **nutritionist** *is an expert in nutrition; she can help you put together a healthy diet that is right for your body's needs.*

Synthesis *means the process of putting something together or making it.*

If something is **fortified** *it has been made stronger (or more nutritious) than normal.*

Although practice and training are important parts of being safe and successful in the game of basketball, you also need to think about what you take into your body. Athletes must be careful to eat a proper blend of nutrients to make sure their bodies and minds perform as well as they possibly can. This doesn't just mean eating healthy foods, but also choosing when to eat, how much to eat, and whether to take dietary supplements. Of course, when you choose a new diet or supplements, you should consult with a **nutritionist**, doctor, or other expert. Don't make up your own nutrition program!

Eating a balanced diet of all the major food groups of the food pyramid (grains, vegetables, fruits, milk, meat and beans) is the best way to fuel your body for athletic activity.

What to Eat

While a balanced diet is important for everyone, it is even more important for athletes. Typically, an athlete has to eat considerably more than other people do. The United States Food and Drug Administration (FDA) suggests that the average American should eat about 2000 calories a day; for a male high school- or college-level basketball player, a 3,000–4,000 calorie diet is more common. There are three main food groups to consider when choosing a diet: carbohydrates, protein, and fats.

CARBOHYDRATES

Carbohydrates are foods rich in a chemical called starch, which is what the body breaks down to get energy. Starchy foods include breads and grains, vegetables such as potatoes, cereal, pasta, and rice. Roughly half an athlete's calories should come from carbohydrates, but you should beware of heavily processed carbohydrates such as sugary foods and white bread made with bleached flour. These foods are quickly broken down into sugars, which the body processes into fats if it does not immediately burn them off. The best carbohydrate choices for an athlete are pasta and whole-grain foods, as well as starchy

Breads and pastas are good sources of carbohydrates, though whole grain products contain more complex carbs than others.

Cholesterol

A lot of bad things have been said about cholesterol—but most of this bad press focuses on LDLs, or low-density lipoproteins, a kind of cholesterol that can clog our blood vessels and make our hearts work harder. Our bodies make this cholesterol out of saturated fats, like those found in animal fat from meats, butter, and whole milk. It is important to know, though, that there is a kind of cholesterol that has a good effect on the body. HDLs, or high-density lipoproteins can be increased as easily as exercising regularly.

vegetables, which have vitamins as well as carbohydrates. A balanced diet avoids the "empty calories" supplied by white bread and sugars.

PROTEIN

Proteins are important chemicals found in all living things; these chemicals are used to perform specific functions inside our body cells. Each protein is a long, folded, chain-like molecule made up of "links" called amino acids. Our bodies can break down proteins into their base amino acids and use them to build new proteins that make up our muscles and bones. For this reason, it is important to eat enough protein to give the body the building blocks it needs to become stronger, especially during exercise. The best sources of proteins are meats and dairy products such as milk or cheese, as well as eggs and certain vegetables (like soy, beans, and rice). To know how much protein to eat, a good rule of thumb is the number of grams should be equal to about one-third of your body weight in pounds. For example, a 200-pound person should have roughly 70 grams of protein per day.

FATS

Lots of times we think of fats as strictly "bad," since eating too much of them is unhealthy. However, fat is an important ingredient needed to make our bodies function correctly. Without fats, we could not absorb certain vitamins efficiently. Our skin and hair also need some amount of fat in order to grow correctly. However, fats should still be eaten in moderation—no more than 70 grams per day. The best sources of fat are vegetable oils, olive oil, and nuts. Many foods contain saturated fats, which lead to the formation of cholesterol and can force your heart to work harder.

It is very important to understand what you are taking into your body. Checking nutrition labels is the best way to know how much fat is in a food or beverage product, for instance.

Dietary Supplements

Many basketball players seek to improve their performance by taking dietary supplements, which are pills or drinks that contain nutrients or chemicals to improve their performance during the game. Dietary supplements do not include illegal performance-enhancing drugs. Instead, they contain vitamins, minerals, or chemicals that help the body use those vitamins more efficiently. When properly used, supplements can improve overall health and performance, but you should always consult a doctor or nutritionist before taking them.

Staying Hydrated

The best diet in the world is no good if you become hydrated. Dehydration occurs when your body doesn't have enough water, leading to fatigue, dizziness, and headaches, all of which can hurt your performance when playing. It's best to carry a bottle of water with you the whole day before a practice or game to make sure you are fully hydrated. In addition, you should be drinking water throughout the game to avoid becoming dehydrated as you sweat; staying fully hydrated has many benefits besides helping your performance in a game. It can help concentration, improve digestive health, and reduce the risk of kidney stones.

Some examples of common supplements include vitamin tablets, creatine, and protein shakes or powder.

VITAMIN TABLETS

We do not always get the vitamins and nutrients we need, usually because our diets are not as balanced as they should be. Sometimes, it's because the foods available to us have been processed in such a way that they lose their nutrients. Also, exhausted soil all over the country means that fruits and vegetables are often not as nutrient-rich as they should be. In many cases, we can get vitamins we need from vitamin supplements. These supplements, usually taken as pills, contain a balanced mixture of vitamins and nutrients known as multivitamins. Sometimes they contain a single vitamin or mineral that our diet is lacking. Be careful when taking vitamin supplements, however, because it is possible to overdose on certain ones. Don't assume that more is always better! And don't forget to always talk to your doctor before beginning supplements of any kind.

CREATINE

Creatine is a specific protein naturally found in your body's muscle cells. When taken in larger doses than is found in the body, creatine has the effect of increasing the rate of protein **synthesis** within your body's cells. You will have more energy to exercise and will see a greater improvement in strength

Dietary supplements can help add to an already balanced diet, but it's important to speak with your doctor before taking any supplement.

and speed when you do. However, putting any chemical into your body can have negative effects, and you should talk to a doctor before starting creatine. Creatine is only suited for adult athletes, though, so young people under the age of 17 should not take it.

PROTEIN SUPPLEMENTS

Getting enough protein from the food you eat can be difficult. Eating protein immediately after a workout is recommended in order to refuel your

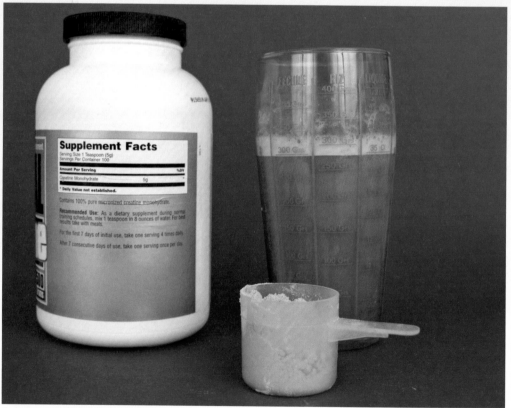

Drinking protein shakes can be a good way to get large amounts of protein after a workout, but they should never be used to replace meals.

Basketball and Alcohol

After a big victory, players may be tempted to celebrate with alcohol. They may also be tempted to use it to ease the pain of defeat. But alcohol intake can interfere with the body's recovery process, and this may interfere with your next game's performance.

It's especially important to avoid any alcohol 24 hours after exercise if you have any soft tissue injuries or bruises. Alcohol and injuries are a bad combination, as alcohol can actually increase swelling and bleeding, delaying the healing process.

body. The problem is, not many people feel up to preparing a meal right after exercising, so protein shakes are often a convenient and healthy choice. Many shakes contain blends of protein, carbohydrates, and fats, and some include vitamins to help balance an athlete's diet. Furthermore, having protein immediately after a workout can help repair the damage sustained by your muscles during exercise. You should always remember that while protein shakes are useful for supplementing your diet, they should never be used to replace meals in significant quantities. Your body still needs plenty of nutrients that it can only get from a balanced diet. No matter how **fortified** a protein shake may be, it cannot adequately replace a real meal. A nutritionist can tell you how to fit protein or supplement shakes into your diet safely and effectively.

Dr. J (1950-)

Julius Erving realized his gift for basketball could be a ticket to a better life. By the time he was ten, he was averaging eleven points a game with his Salvation Army team, and he went on to play on his high school team. From there, he went to all-county and all-Long Island teams competing in statewide tournaments. He got the nickname "the Doctor" while he was still in high school, and his teammates would later change this to "Dr. J."

The basketball coach at Julius's high school introduced him to the basketball coach at the University of Massachusetts, and Julius entered college there after his high school graduation. At Massachusetts, Julius broke freshman records for scoring and rebounding, leading his team through an undefeated season. The next year, he had the second best rebound tally in the country. Over the summer, he joined an NCAA all-star team touring Western Europe and the Soviet Union, and he was voted most valuable player on this tour.

Julius left the university to go professional after his junior year. He is one of only seven players in the history of NCAA basketball to average over 20 points and 20 rebounds per game. He began his professional career with the Virginia Squires of the American Basketball Association. The ABA was fighting an uphill battle to gain the same recognition enjoyed by the more established National Basketball Association (NBA). Dr. J, as his fans now called him, did more than anyone else to win that recognition for the new association. In his first pro season, he ranked sixth in the ABA in scoring, third in rebounding. He was voted ABA Rookie of the Year at the close of the season. The following year, he averaged 31.9 points per game. In 1973, Dr. J scored 47 points in a single game. People were saying he was one of the greatest basketball players of all time.

In the 1974 season, Erving suffered from knee pains and had to wear special braces on the court, but that didn't stop him from another spectacular season. On his 25th birthday, he scored 57 points against San Diego.

After being voted Most Valuable Player in the ABA from 1974 to 1976, Dr. J moved to the Philadelphia 76ers of the National Basketball Association. He remained in Philadelphia for the last eleven years of his pro basketball career, leading the 76ers to an NBA championship in 1983.

When Dr. J finally retired in 1987, he had scored over 30,000 points in his professional career; he is one of only three players in the history of the game to achieve this feat. After retiring from professional basketball, Julius Erving became a commentator for NBC. He is now a successful businessman—but his memory as a basketball superstar lives on in the Basketball Hall of Fame.

6
The Dangers of Performance-Enhancing Drugs

Understanding the Words

Infertility *means the inability to produce sperm or eggs; someone who is infertile cannot have biological children.*

An electrolyte *is a salt or mineral that conducts electrical impulses in the body, which is necessary for good health.*

If you have a potassium deficiency, *you lack enough potassium— one of the body's necessary electrolytes—to be healthy.*

Hormones *are the chemicals in your body that control and regulate the activity of many body systems.*

Insomnia *is a condition where you are unable to fall asleep.*

Hypertension *is the medical term for high blood pressure.*

Hallucinations *are when a person sees something that is not really there.*

Sadly, not all aspects of basketball are glamorous and exciting. If you follow sports, you have most likely heard of athletes who use steroids and the controversy that surrounds them. By definition, performance-enhancing

Potential Negative Side Effects of Steroids

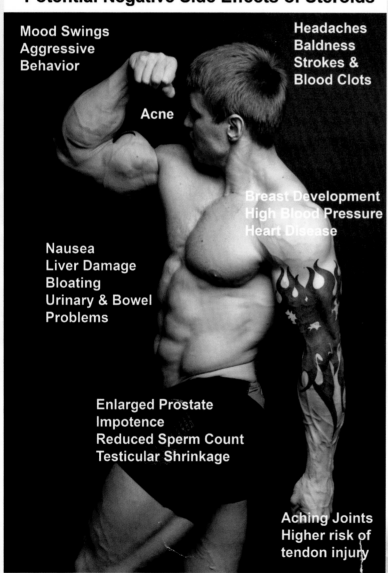

Mood Swings
Aggressive
Behavior

Headaches
Baldness
Strokes &
Blood Clots

Acne

Breast Development
High Blood Pressure
Heart Disease

Nausea
Liver Damage
Bloating
Urinary & Bowel
Problems

Enlarged Prostate
Impotence
Reduced Sperm Count
Testicular Shrinkage

Aching Joints
Higher risk of
tendon injury

Steroids can cause many unwelcome side effects in young male athletes. Some side effects seen in women who take steroids include a deepened voice, increase in facial and body hair, reduced breast size and menstrual problems.

drugs are any form of chemicals that are taken in order to improve physical strength. While this may seem like a foolproof way to succeed on the court, it is actually much more complicated than that. Not only are there legal consequences, but there are also health issues.

Ben Johnson, Canadian Olympic sprinter, Barry Bonds of the San Francisco Giants, and Floyd Landis, winner of the 2006 Tour de France are all amazingly accomplished athletes—but that's not all they have in common. All their careers have been tarnished by their use of performance-enhancing drugs. Landis, for example, had his title stripped from him and was dismissed from his cycling team after a urine test came back positive for high amounts of testosterone. Johnson, who won the 1987 World Championships and 1988 Summer Olympics, had his gold medal ripped from him just days after winning because he tested positive for anabolic steroids. And Bonds was indicted by the federal grand jury and charged with supplying steroids to other athletes; even though he has 7 MVP awards and is known as one of the best major league baseball players ever, he has said that no team will pick him up now for even a minimum salary.

Anabolic-Androgenic Steroids

Anabolic-androgenic steroids are usually taken to increase muscle mass. The main natural steroid produced by the body is testosterone, which causes muscle mass and male secondary characteristics such as facial hair. Athletes take steroids such as methyltestosterone and oxymetholone in order to build muscle and recover from workouts. Since these drugs are illegal for athletes to use, beginning in 2002, "designer" drugs such as tetrahydrogestrinone (THG) have been created that allow athletes to be tested for steroid use without registering positive.

Many of these drugs are so new that they have not been tested thoroughly. Early indications are that these steroids may have serious side effects in men that range from baldness to growth of breasts, shrunken testicles, and infertility. Women tend to develop increased body hair, a deeper voice, and baldness. Both men and women may develop severe acne, liver abnormalities and tumors, cholesterol abnormalities, aggressive behavior, drug dependence, and future health risks. As of today, taking anabolic-

What Professionals Have to Say About Steroids

Rudy Gay of the Memphis Grizzlies:
"In our sport steroids would hurt you more than help you. You wouldn't get much use out of them because I think steroids would affect your longevity in the NBA. The way steroids hurt your body there is no way you could use them and have a long career."

Mike Freeman, CBSSports.com national columnist:
"Because there is so much running and jumping . . . along with a lengthy season and numerous games . . . steroids would speed the breaking down of knees and other joints."

Gerald Green of the Dallas Mavericks:
"Steroids make you too big. You need to be fluid to play basketball. You'd be too slow if you used steroids in the NBA. You need to be agile to play basketball on this level, not so bulked up."

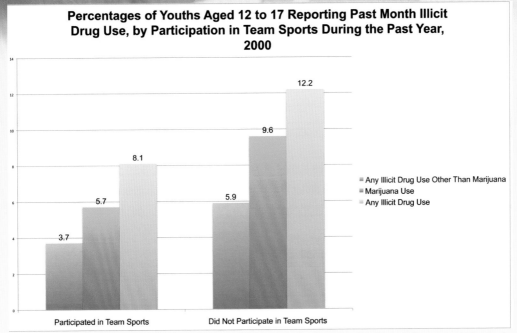

Percentages of Youths Aged 12 to 17 Reporting Past Month Illicit Drug Use, by Participation in Team Sports During the Past Year, 2000

While some young athletes do try to enhance their performance with illegal drug use, this study from the National Household Survey on Drug Abuse shows that participation in sports tends to reduce drug use among teenagers.

androgenic steroids is illegal for enhancing sports performance, and they are outlawed in competition.

Diuretics

Diuretics are a class of drugs that increases urine production. Some athletes also believe that diuretics help them pass drug testing, since they dilute the urine. However, taking diuretics can upset they body's **electrolyte** balance and lead to dehydration. Taking diuretics such as Acetazolamide (Diamox) can lead to muscle cramps, exhaustion, dizziness, **potassium deficiency**, a drop in blood pressure, and even death.

Androstenedione

Androstenedione is a hormone produced naturally by the adrenal glands, ovaries, and testes, which is then converted to testosterone and estradiol, the human sex **hormones**. Artificially-produced androstenedione is a controlled substance that is illegal in competition in the United States, though it is still being sold.

Scientific evidence suggests that androstenodione doesn't promote muscle growth, and it has several risks. In men, side effects include acne, diminished sperm production, shrunken testicles, and enlargement of breasts. In women, the drug causes acne and masculinization, such as growth of facial hair. Androstenedione has also been shown to increase the chances of a heart attack and stroke because it causes buildup of bad cholesterol.

Stimulants

Stimulants are a class of drugs that increases breathing rate, heart rate, and blood circulation. Athletes believe these drugs stimulate their central nervous system, allowing them to perform better. Stimulants such as caffeine, cold remedies, and street drugs (cocaine and methamphetamine) can promote alertness, suppress appetite, and increase aggressiveness. However, these drugs can also make an athlete have difficulty concentrating, as well as produce **insomnia**, nervousness, and irritability. Athletes can even become psychologically addicted. Other side effects include weight loss, tremors, heart rate abnormalities, **hypertension**, **hallucinations**, and heart attacks.

Over-the-Counter Drugs

Besides these dangerous and often illegal drugs, athletes also use painkillers and sedatives to enhance their performance. Painkillers allow athletes to operate with a higher level of pain tolerance, while sedatives can allow athletes to concentrate under stressful situations. However, both these drugs can also decrease performance—and they can disqualify an athlete from competing if they're detected in her bloodstream.

The Consequences of Performance-Enhancing Drug Use

Basketball players, like all athletes, are often looking for a greater competitive edge to gain fame, acclaim, or an award and prize. However, there is no

Both the NBA and NCAA test players for drug use, including the use of banned performance-enhancing drugs.

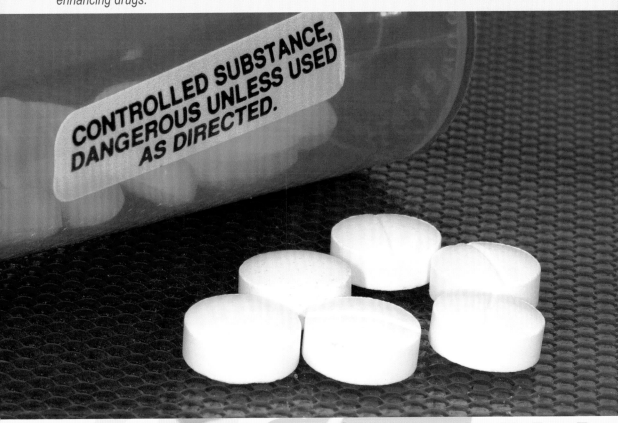

Shooting for the Stars

Teen basketball player Kristine Lalonde knew she didn't need performance-enhancing drugs to excel in her sport, and the summer of 2008 proved she has what it takes. She was last cut from the U18 Junior National Team, was invited to the Nike All Canada Camp, earned her fourth gold National Championship medal from Team Ontario, was selected to attend and train at Basketball Canada's National Elite Development Academy (NEDA) for the 2008–09 school year, and was honored at the Ontario Basketball Hall of Fame.

Kristine played three years of high school basketball in Sudbury, Ontario. She made the varsity team as a ninth grader and helped her school win three city championships, three regional championships, and advance to the provincial championships three times. Kristine then went on to play for the University of Vermont. She says her motto is, "Shoot for the stars!"

magical concoction that will automatically bring these rewards. Instead, these performance-enhancing drugs tend to have many adverse side effects that could harm the body and its performance more than they help.

The NBA has banned the use of anabolic steroids for nonmedical reasons, and the National Collegiate Athletic Association, or NCAA, also has very strict consequences for the use of this drug. The NCAA sponsors two drug-testing programs, and both are required for every institution that is part of the association. Athletes are tested during NCAA Championships as well as randomly throughout the year. Not only are college athletes forbidden from taking steroids, but they are also not allowed to take a variety of other drugs: anti-estrogens, diuretics, stimulants, peptide hormones, analogues, as well as any and all street drugs. In fact, the NCAA's list of banned drugs includes more substances than those that are illegal according to federal law. If a NCAA athlete tests positive for a drug test, the student is banned from competing in any intercollegiate sport for an entire academic year, and loses one of his four years of eligibility. On the second offense, however, the athlete is banned indefinitely from all NCAA sports with no exceptions.

Celtics player Larry Bird once said, "I've got a theory that if you give 100 percent all of the time, somehow things will work out in the end." It's that dedication to your sport that is the true secret to success when it comes to basketball. There are no shortcuts!

Further Reading

Dunphy, Fran. 2009. *The Baffled Parent's Guide to Great Basketball Plays.* International Marine/Ragged Mountain Press: Thomaston, ME.

Gamble, Paul. 2010. *Strength and Conditioning for Team Sports: Sport-Specific Physical Preparation for High Performance.* Routledge: New York, NY.

Gandolfi, Giorgio. 2009. *The Complete Book of Offensive Basketball Drills: Game-Changing Drills from Around the World.* McGraw Hill: Columbus, OH.

Kolb, Joe. 2002. *Get Fit Now for High School Basketball: Strength and Conditioning for Ultimate Performance on the Court.* Hatherleigh Press: Long Island City, NY.

Price, Robert. 2006. *The Ultimate Guide to Weight Training for Basketball.* Sportsworkout.com.

Find Out More on the Internet

American Academy of Orthopaedic Surgeons-
Basketball Injury Prevention
orthoinfo.aaos.org/topic.cfm?topic=A00177

Better Basketball
www.betterbasketball.com

National Basketball Association
www.nba.com

Sports Injury Clinic
www.sportsinjuryclinic.net

Youth Basketball Tips
www.youth-basketball-tips.com

Disclaimer

The websites listed on this page were active at the time of publication. The publisher is not responsible for websites that have changed their address or discontinued operation since the date of publication. The publisher will review and update the websites upon each reprint.

Bibliography

AllSands, "James Naismith," www.allsands.com/entertainment/people/jamesnaismith_byx_gn.htm (3 February 2010).

Basketball Plays & Tips, "Basketball Stretches," www.basketball-plays-and-tips.com/basketball-stretch.html (5 February 2010).

Body Building, "Fun," www.bodybuilding.com/fun/md49.htm (5 February 2010).

Breakthrough Basketball, "Basketball Basics," www.breakthroughbasketball.com/basics/basics.html (6 February 2010).

Exercise Goals, "Basketball Weightlifting," www.exercisegoals.com/basketball-weight-lifting.html (5 February 2010).

Fernando, Anthony, "Michael Phelps' Five Secrets of Success," www.anthonyfernando.com/2008/08/18/michael-phelps-five-secrets-of-success (5 February 2010).

Freeman, Mike, CBS Sports, "Steroids in NBA? Bulk Doesn't Translate in Fluid Game," www.cbssports.com/nba/story/10648024/1 (3 February 2010).

Hartgens, F. and H. Kulpers, PubMed, "Effects of Androgenic-Anabolic Steroids in Athletes," www.ncbi.nlm.nih.gov/pubmed/15248788 (6 February 2010).

NBA, "History of Women's Basketball," www.wnba.com/about_us/jenkins_feature.html (4 February 2010).

NCAA, "Drug Testing," www.ncaa.org/wps/portal/ncaahome?WCM_GLOBAL_CONTEXT=/ncaa/ncaa/media+and+events/press+room/current+issues/drug+testing (6 February 2010).

Romow Sports Blog, "Lebron James' Biography," www.romow.com/sports-blog/lebron-james-biography (5 February 2010).

Sports Medicine, "Anabolic Steroids," sportsmedicine.about.com/od/performanceenhancingdrugs/a/AnabolicSteroid.htm (7 February 2010).

"Sports Superstitions," www.sportssuperstitions.net/page3.html (5 February 2010).

ThinkQuest, "Basketball History," library.thinkquest.org/10615/no-frames/basketball/history.html (5 February 2010).

Top-Tenz, "Top 10 Sports Figures Whose Careers are Tarnished by Steroids," www.toptenz.net/top-10-sports-figures-steroids.php (7 February 2010).

Youth Sports, "Sports Psychology," www.youthsportspsychology.com/youth_sports_psychology_blog/?p=273 (5 February 2010).

Index

Picture Credits

Creative Commons Attribution 2.0 Generic
  aaronisnotcool: pg. 43

Creative Commons Attribution-ShareAlike
2.0 Generic
  JoeJohnson2: pg. 12

Dreamstime.com:
  alerijs Vinogradovs p. 65
  Clifford Farrugia p. 76
  Margreet De Groot p. 71
  Martin Vonka p. 63
  Sebastian Kaulitzki pp. 59, 61, 64
  Stephen Vanhorn p. 73
  Tan Wei Ming p. 67

Fotolia.com:
  Andrei vishnyakov: p. 86
  AndreasG p. 20
  Dana S. Rothstein p. 87

Brian Erickson p. 27
Ken Mellott p. 56
Gheorghe Roman p. 17
Konstantin Yuganov pp. pp. 9, 25, 39,
  55, 69, 81
ktsdesign pp. 9, 25, 39, 55, 69, 81
Leonid Dorfman pp. 8, 24, 38, 54, 68,
  80
Lorraine Swanson p. 31
mark edwards p. 28
Michael Chamberlin p. 26
Nicholas Moore p. 18
Scott Maxwell p. 35
TheSupe87 p. 20
Vicky Andriotis p. 75
zimmytws p. 36

United States Air Force
  Sara Csurill: pg. 51

United States Navy
  Kyle Carlstrom: pg. 46

To the best knowledge of the publisher, all images not specifically credited are in the
public domain. If any image has been inadvertently uncredited, please notify Harding
House Publishing Service, 220 Front Street, Vestal, New York 13850, so that credit can
be given in future printings.

About the Author and the Consultants

Gabrielle Vanderhoof is a former competitive figure skater. She now works in publishing and public relations. This is her first time writing for Mason Crest.

Susan Saliba, Ph.D., is a senior associate athletic trainer and a clinical instructor at the University of Virginia in Charlottesville, Virginia. A certified athletic trainer and licensed physical therapist, Dr. Saliba provides sports medicine care, including prevention, treatment, and rehabilitation for the varsity athletes at the university. Dr. Saliba is a member of the national Athletic Trainers' Association Educational Executive Committee and its Clinical Education Committee.

Eric Small, M.D., a Harvard-trained sports medicine physician, is a nationally recognized expert in the field of sports injuries, nutritional supplements, and weight management programs. He is author of *Kids & Sports* (2002) and is Assistant Clinical professor of pediatrics, Orthopedics, and Rehabilitation Medicine at Mount Sinai School of Medicine in New York. He is also Director of the Sports Medicine Center for Young Athletes at Blythedale Children's Hospital in Valhalla, New York. Dr. Small has served on the American Academy of Pediatrics Committee on Sports Medicine, where he develops national policy regarding children's medical issues and sports.